The Library of Sexual Health™

GENITAL HERPES

GREG SAULMON

The Rosen Publishing Group, Inc., New York

Published in 2007 by The Rosen Publishing Group, Inc.
29 East 21st Street, New York, NY 10010

Library of Congress Cataloging-in-Publication Data

Saulmon, Greg.
Genital herpes/Greg Saulmon.
    p. cm.—(The library of sexual health)
Includes bibliographical references and index.
ISBN-13: 978-1-4042-0907-7
ISBN-10: 1-4042-0907-7 (library binding)
1. Herpes genitalis—Juvenile literature. I. Title. II. Series.
RC203.H45S28 2006
616.95'18—dc22

                                                    2006002095

Manufactured in the United States of America

CONTENTS

INTRODUCTION

Genital herpes is one of the most common sexually transmitted diseases (STDs) in the world. Although it's not fatal, it has no cure and it can be very difficult to detect. According to the Centers for Disease Control and Prevention (CDC), at least 45 million Americans over the age of twelve—that's one out of every five teens and adults in the United States—currently suffer from the infection. And that number may be much higher since many people don't even realize they are infected.

Teenagers represent the fastest-growing group of people with genital herpes. This may occur because, even though the disease is so common, there are many myths about how it spreads and who can get it. The fact is that

Helping Advance Women's Health

Vaccine Against Herpes

We are currently enrolling for a preventative vaccine against Herpes.

The study is open to women ages 18-30, who have never had any mouth or genital lesions. This is a 20 month study.

Features include financial compensation for time and travel: $40.00 per visit for a total of $360.00 if all visits are completed.

Anyone who has sex is at risk for Herpes. For more information on how you can help, contact June or Maria at the Clinical Studies office at URI.

Help Prevent Herpes in Women

There is no cure for genital herpes. However, scientists are working to develop a vaccine that could help prevent more people from contracting the disease. The ad, above, is a call for female participants in a vaccine research study.

anyone who is sexually active is at risk. Whether you have had a number of sexual relationships or just "fooled around" with one person, all it takes is one contact with the herpes virus to contract the disease for life.

This book explains what genital herpes is, what its symptoms are, and how it's passed from one person to another. You'll learn facts about testing, treatment options, and how to deal with your feelings if you have genital herpes.

Most important, though, this book will teach you how to keep yourself and the people you care about safe. Preventing genital herpes—whether you choose abstinence or methods for safer sex—is in your hands. Genital herpes may be extremely common. But that doesn't mean you are powerless to help stop its spread.

CHAPTER ONE

What Is Genital Herpes?

L ike many diseases, genital herpes is caused by a virus. Other STDs caused by viruses include genital warts; hepatitis; and the human immunodeficiency virus (HIV), which causes acquired immunodeficiency syndrome (AIDS).

Viruses are the smallest living things in the world. They are so small, in fact, that even two million of them lined up in a row would measure less than a half inch (about 1.3 centimeters). The "host cells" of larger organisms, such as animals and people, provide the food and energy that viruses need to survive.

Viruses also use host cells for another important function—reproduction. On their own, viruses are not able to multiply. But they can use structures within a host cell to produce more viruses. When an infected cell bursts open, it can release hundreds or even thousands of virus particles. And what do all these particles do? They look for other cells to infect.

THE HERPES VIRUS

Viruses cause each of the eight different kinds of herpes. These include diseases such as mononucleosis ("mono") and cytomegalovirus (CMV). One virus even causes shingles, a disease that's related to chicken pox. These aren't STDs, however. The kind of herpes this book will discuss—caused by the herpes simplex virus (sometimes shortened to "HSV")—can be passed through sexual activity.

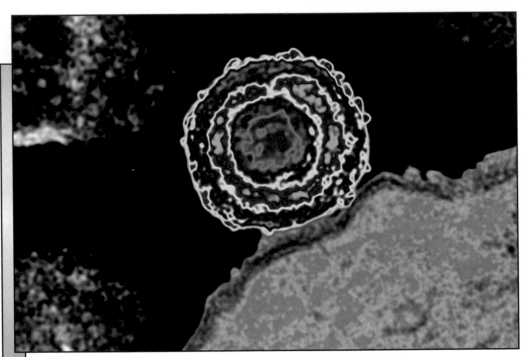

Viruses are the smallest living things in the world. In this picture, the multicolored herpes simplex virus prepares to enter and infect the green-and-orange "host cell" of a larger organism.

Herpes simplex actually refers to two different viruses: herpes simplex 1 (HSV-1) and herpes simplex 2 (HSV-2). The fact that there are two different herpes simplex viruses causes a lot of confusion. The structure of the two viruses is extremely similar—only complicated tests can tell them apart. Still, people view the two viruses very differently.

Have you ever had a cold sore or fever blister? If so, then you most likely have had HSV-1 (sometimes called

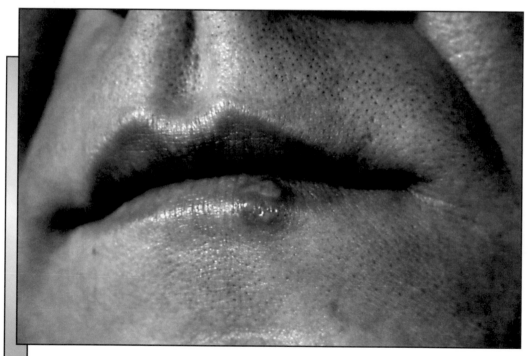

Herpes simplex 1 (HSV-1) causes painful blisters (known as cold sores and fever blisters) in or around the mouth.

oral herpes because it affects the area around the mouth). Almost all people get cold sores at one time or another. Since cold sores are so common, most people don't see HSV-1 in a negative light. In fact, many don't realize it's a disease at all or know that it's a form of herpes.

The other kind of herpes, HSV-2, is passed through vaginal, anal, or oral sex. This is the kind that's typically called genital herpes. In general, HSV-1 affects the mouth and HSV-2 affects the genitals, but people can get HSV-1 on their genitals and HSV-2 in their mouth. Since HSV-2 is passed through sexual contact, people are more likely to attach a stigma to the disease. This means that people may assume that someone with genital herpes has poor morals, or that he or she is "easy" or has had many sexual partners. But that is not necessarily the case. The truth is that anybody who has any type of sex can get genital herpes. Even condoms are not 100-percent effective in stopping the spread of the disease.

The good news is that genital herpes isn't fatal. And it doesn't automatically get worse over time. The bad news is that genital herpes can't be cured. Once you're infected, you have the disease for the rest of your life. The virus lives in your body's nerve endings. This is a place where the immune system is unable to detect and fight the virus. Every once in a while, the virus is reactivated—it "wakes up," travels through the nerve pathways in your body, and causes an outbreak. That may be how herpes got its name. The word "herpes" is Greek for "to creep."

BLISTERS, BUMPS, AND BURNING— THE SYMPTOMS OF GENITAL HERPES

Many people don't realize that not everyone with genital herpes shows the same symptoms or even has symptoms. In addition, symptoms aren't permanent. You can't see or notice them all the time. Instead, they tend to come and go over a person's lifetime. It can be hard to tell exactly

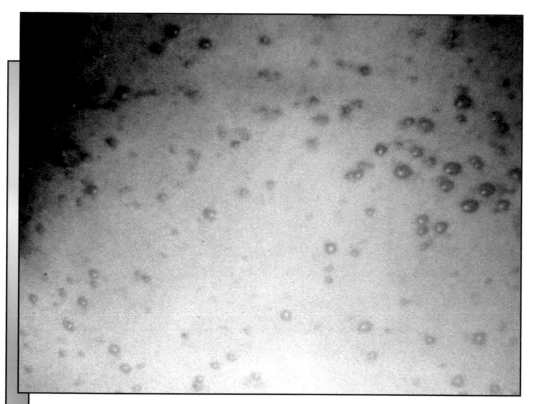

The symptoms of herpes can take many forms. Sometimes, as with cold sores, there is just a single blister. Other times, a number of blisters will form, and the virus can resemble a rash.

when you got genital herpes. Symptoms can first appear between three and ten days after you've been exposed to the virus. But in some cases, symptoms don't show up for months or even years. Some people with genital herpes can go their whole lives without ever having an outbreak or showing any symptoms at all.

A genital herpes outbreak often begins as an itching or burning feeling in the infected area. For both genders, this can be on the upper thighs or buttocks, or around the anus. For men, it can also be on the penis or scrotum (and the surrounding area). For women, it can also be around or inside the vagina.

The itching and burning feeling signals the progression to come. After a few days (or sometimes just a few hours) small red bumps begin to appear in the infected area. The bumps may turn into watery blisters, which become painful open sores (also called lesions). These blisters are one of the most noticeable symptoms of genital herpes. Then, the sores tend to ooze fluid. This is the stage when the disease is most likely to be passed on to another person. Once scabs form on the sores, they usually heal in a few days or weeks.

At first, many people don't realize that these symptoms are a sign of genital herpes. A lot of people think the small red bumps are ingrown hairs, pimples, bug bites, or just a rash. Men might think it's jock itch, and women might mistake the signs of an outbreak for razor burn or a yeast infection.

These sores may be the calling card of genital herpes, but there are other symptoms as well. Many who have the disease experience pain or a burning sensation when they urinate. Others have flu-like symptoms, such as a fever and swollen glands—especially during their first outbreak. Genital herpes can also cause headaches and muscle pain. Some women experience vaginal discharge. In addition to painful urination, an outbreak can cause severe aching and itching if a woman is having her period.

An outbreak of genital herpes can be a very uncomfortable experience. During any outbreak, the entire genital area is likely to feel very tender or painful. However, a person's first outbreak is usually his or her worst. Some people have four to five outbreaks each year. Others may have only one a year, or one their whole life. Over time, outbreaks can become less frequent. Later outbreaks tend to be shorter and less severe, and the sores may heal more quickly.

Genital herpes generally affects the organs of the male and female reproductive systems.

Ten Facts About Genital Herpes

1. The two types of herpes are HSV-1 and HSV-2. HSV-1 typically causes oral herpes (cold sores). HSV-2 typically causes genital herpes (but both can affect the mouth and genitals).

2. About 45 million Americans over the age of twelve have genital herpes. That's one out of every five adults and teens.

3. A person's first outbreak of genital herpes usually happens three to ten days after he or she is exposed to the virus.

4. Genital herpes is not fatal.

5. There is no cure for genital herpes. Once you are infected, the virus lives in your body for the rest of your life.

6. As many as one million new cases of genital herpes occur in the United States each year.

7. About 90 percent of the people infected with genital herpes do not know that they have the disease.

8. Not all people with genital herpes show symptoms. They can spread the disease even if they don't have any sores or blisters.

9. Genital herpes is passed through direct skin-to-skin contact. You can't catch it from a toilet seat or hot tub.

10. Having genital herpes makes it easier to get the HIV virus, or to pass HIV to another person.

Outbreaks can happen at any time, but there may be triggers. For example, some people have reported that stress and sun exposure seem to cause outbreaks. Others believe that eating certain foods—such as chocolate or walnuts—can lead to the appearance of genital herpes blisters and sores.

CHAPTER TWO

Infection and Symptoms

Genital herpes is passed through direct skin-to-skin contact with someone who's infected. It can't be spread through the air, so you can't get it just by being near someone who's infected—even if he or she coughs on you.

HOW IT'S SPREAD

The easiest way to catch genital herpes is by touching the blisters, sores, or rash of someone who's infected and having an outbreak. That can mean having sexual contact with someone who has open sores on or around his or her genitals or anus. High amounts of the virus live in the fluid of open sores, so coming into contact with the fluid puts a person at high risk for catching the infection.

Even though genital herpes is more contagious when a person has an outbreak of open sores, the infection can also spread through sex when there are no symptoms present. There's even evidence that most cases of genital herpes are passed when the infected partner isn't showing

Genital herpes is spread only through direct skin-to-skin contact. It is not spread through the air, so you can't catch it by being in a crowd, shaking hands, or just being near someone who has it.

any symptoms. This probably occurs for two reasons. First, most people don't know that they have genital herpes. Since not everyone experiences outbreaks or shows symptoms, an infected person may believe that he or she is perfectly healthy. Therefore, someone may not know to inform his or her partner of the risk. Second, people often assume that they'll be able to tell if their partner has genital herpes. But you can't tell if someone has genital herpes just by looking at him or her. And that means you could catch genital herpes from anyone.

People with genital herpes are often most contagious during the first six months after they contract the disease. During this period, the rate of viral shedding is at its highest. Viral shedding means that the virus has crept to the surface of the skin and is ready to be passed to others.

Anyone who is sexually active can get genital herpes. But that doesn't mean that only people who have vaginal intercourse are at risk. Being sexually active means having any kind of contact with another person's genitals or anus— even if there's no penetration. It is also possible to get herpes if someone with a cold sore performs oral sex. In such circumstances, HSV-1, typically known as oral herpes, could develop on the other person's genitals. Another fact to be aware of is that it is possible for you to spread your herpes to another part of your body. For example, if you touch a cold sore and then touch your eye, your next outbreak could occur on your eye.

Myths and Facts

MYTH: You can get genital herpes from objects like toilet seats.
FACT: The herpes virus needs the protection of its host to survive. It dies very quickly once it is exposed to air. Doctors have never been able to link a case of genital herpes to exposure to a toilet seat or any other object.

MYTH: It's easy to tell if someone has genital herpes.
FACT: A lot of the time, a person with genital herpes doesn't show symptoms. Blisters and lesions appear during outbreaks—but these outbreaks may only happen a few times during a person's life. Some people with genital herpes may never have an outbreak. Whether or not someone is showing symptoms, he or she can still pass the infection on to others.

MYTH: Genital herpes is transmitted only during vaginal intercourse.
FACT: Genital herpes can be transmitted during vaginal intercourse—but oral sex and anal sex are also very common ways for the infection to spread. Also remember: genital herpes can be passed on to another person even when blisters or sores are not visible.

MYTH: Having genital herpes means that you can never have children.
FACT: Genital herpes does not cause infertility. A woman with genital herpes can still get pregnant, and a man with genital herpes can still make a woman pregnant. However, a woman with genital herpes can pass the disease to her baby during childbirth.

MYTH: The only people who get genital herpes are people who "sleep around."
FACT: Genital herpes is one of the most common STDs. So, you can catch it even if you have sexual contact with just one person. Your chances of getting genital herpes increases with the number of sexual partners you have.

GENITAL HERPES AND YOUR HEALTH

Although it's not fatal, genital herpes is not a disease to take lightly. The fact that there's no cure means that the disease lasts a lifetime. A person will always be at risk for outbreaks that may be quite painful. The infection can be severe in people with weak immune systems. In rare cases, they may even need to be hospitalized during an outbreak (especially if it's their first one).

Genital herpes is usually not very dangerous during pregnancy. According to the American Social Health

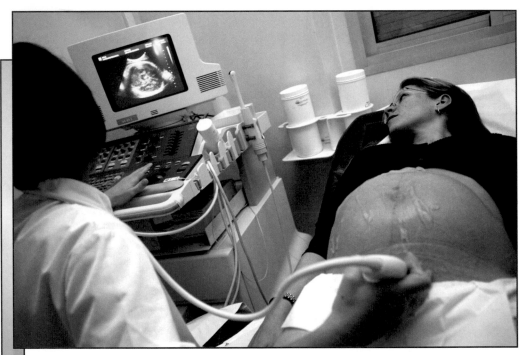

Doctors use ultrasound to check the health of unborn babies. Genital herpes may not be risky for a mother, but it can cause complications and even death for her baby.

Association (ASHA), less than 0.1 percent of babies born in the United States each year get neonatal herpes. Although it is somewhat rare, a woman who has an active genital herpes outbreak during childbirth can pass the infection to her baby. This likelihood is greater if the woman caught the infection late into her pregnancy, or if it is the woman's first outbreak. Because of the risk to the baby's health, most doctors perform a cesarean section when a woman with a genital herpes outbreak is ready to give birth.

Of the few babies that become infected with the virus, half either die or end up with severe brain damage. A baby that catches genital herpes during childbirth is more likely to come down with meningitis, a serious infection that affects the membranes surrounding the brain and spinal cord. Babies with genital herpes are also at a higher risk for problems such as severe rashes, blindness and other vision problems, seizures, and encephalitis (inflammation of the brain).

Doctors and scientists have begun to warn of a link between genital herpes and HIV, the virus that causes AIDS. HIV is spread through bodily fluids and through breaks in the skin. Having open sores can make it easier for a person to catch HIV. Fluid (such as blood or semen) containing the HIV virus could enter another person's body through an open sore. A person with HIV is more likely to give HIV to others if he or she also has genital herpes.

CHAPTER THREE

Testing and Treatment

Genital herpes is not always easy to diagnose. Since the symptoms can be so similar to an ingrown hair, pimple, or rash, many people may not bother to visit their doctors. In between outbreaks, the disease can be difficult to detect, even through laboratory testing.

TAKING THE TEST

In most cases, a doctor examining a patient during an outbreak can make a preliminary visual diagnosis. But most doctors will order follow-up tests to confirm whether the patient has genital herpes or not. When open sores are present, a doctor can take a sample from a sore and send it to a lab for testing. This type of test, known as a viral culture test, is the most accurate test available for the diagnosis of genital herpes.

How does the viral culture test work? After the sample is taken from a sore (by swabbing or scraping), it is combined with other healthy cells. After a day or two, a lab technician examines the cells to see how they have changed. If the technician observes changes showing that the virus has grown, the patient is diagnosed as having genital herpes.

Viral culture tests work best during the early stages of an outbreak—especially if it's the patient's first outbreak. During this period, larger amounts of the virus are present in each sore, so it's easier for the doctor to collect a good sample. It is more difficult to collect a sample once sores

Not all people who have genital herpes show symptoms. Getting tested is the only way to know for sure if you have the disease. With viral culture tests, samples are examined under a microscope to check for the herpes virus.

have begun to heal. Therefore, it's always important to get tested right away.

When no symptoms of genital herpes are present, diagnosis is more difficult. Since there are no sores from which to collect a sample, viral culture tests are not an option. Instead, doctors use blood tests. These tests don't detect active genital herpes infection. They work by detecting antibodies to the virus in the patient's blood. Antibodies are produced by the immune system and are the body's way of fighting infection. So, if a blood test shows that the patient has antibodies for the genital herpes virus, it means the patient's body had developed the antibodies to fight off the virus. That means he or she was infected with the virus at some point.

A drawback to some blood testing is that it does not show whether the antibodies are for HSV-1 or HSV-2. So, a positive test only means that the person has been infected with the herpes virus—it doesn't reveal whether the person has oral or genital herpes. There are now tests available that differentiate between HSV-1 and HSV-2, but they tend to be more expensive. A downside to these tests is that the location of the infection is not identified.

AFTER THE DIAGNOSIS

There is no cure for genital herpes. Once infected, you have the infection for the rest of your life. There are treatments, however, that can help you cope. Many people live full and happy lives with this STD.

Medications called antiviral drugs are among the most common and effective treatments. Three types of antiviral drugs are acyclovir (Zovirax), valacyclovir (Valtrex), and famciclovir (Famvir). These drugs make it harder for the virus to reproduce itself, shortening the length of an outbreak and making symptoms less severe.

For a person's first outbreak, doctors usually recommend taking antiviral drugs for seven to ten days. The drugs work best if the person begins taking them within twenty-four hours of the first symptoms of an outbreak. If all the sores haven't healed after ten days, treatment may be extended.

In some cases, antiviral drugs are taken in small doses every day to prevent symptoms. This is called suppressive therapy. It is usually prescribed for someone who has already had genital herpes for a while. The goal of this treatment is to reduce the likelihood

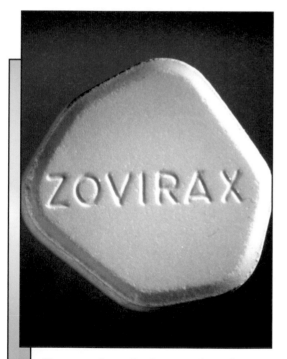

Drugs such as Zovirax can be taken in small doses each day to promote healing and decrease pain and itching. However, these drugs only help ease genital herpes' symptoms; there is no cure for the disease.

of an outbreak. It seems to work. According to research on antiviral drugs and genital herpes, people who take the drugs daily may experience outbreaks much less frequently. About 25 percent of patients who use suppressive therapy never experience outbreaks again.

Suppressive therapy can also make a person less likely to spread the disease. It can't completely stop the risk of transmission, however. No matter what kind of drug therapy a person with genital herpes uses, there's always a chance of spreading the disease to other people through sexual contact.

TAKING CARE OF YOURSELF

In addition to taking the drugs that your doctor prescribes, you can take steps to make an outbreak a little easier to endure. First of all, do not use over-the-counter creams. In order to heal, sores need air. Using petroleum jelly or other oil-based lotions and ointments may feel soothing, but they can actually slow the healing process by keeping air from reaching the sore.

For some people, warm baths and showers (up to three or four a day) can provide a temporary escape from the pain. Just be sure to dry any sores completely afterward. A good way to do this is to use a hairdryer on a low or cool setting. But be careful not to burn yourself.

Loose-fitting cotton clothes are the best choice during outbreaks, especially when it comes to underwear. Cotton

Managing Stress

A lot of people find that stress triggers genital herpes outbreaks. How can you keep stress under control? Here are some things to try:

- **Get adequate rest.** If you're not getting enough sleep, you're more likely to get stressed out.

- **Eat right.** This doesn't mean you have to go on a diet. Just make sure that you eat a healthy balance of foods each day.

- **Get moving.** Exercise is a great way to blow off steam. Pick a sport or activity you like so that you'll be motivated to keep up with it.

- **Kick back.** Make time for deep breathing, meditation, or yoga—or any other activity that helps you relax. This can be a great way to beat stress.

Meditation and yoga can be effective ways to relax and relieve stress. During meditation, repeating a single word over and over again while sitting very still can help you focus.

underwear allows air to reach sores, speeding up the healing process.

Whether you try any or all of these strategies, here are some tips for keeping an outbreak under control:

- Keep sores clean and dry. This helps your body fight against other infections.

- Don't touch your sores. If you do, be sure to wash your hands with warm soap and water right away. This can help you avoid spreading sores to other parts of your body.
- When you have an outbreak, don't have sex—of any kind. From the time symptoms first appear to the time when all sores have healed completely, it's best to avoid any sexual contact. If you choose to have sex in between outbreaks, use a condom and other barrier methods to prevent herpes transmission.

RESEARCH IN THE WORKS

It might be unrealistic to expect scientists to find a cure for genital herpes. Instead, researchers are focusing on the next best thing: a vaccine against HSV-2. A vaccine would not help those who already have the disease. It could, however, keep many people from catching HSV-2 in the future.

In the United States, the National Institutes of Health (NIH) is currently testing a vaccine. Even if scientists prove that the vaccine works, though, it won't be available to the public right away. All drugs sold legally in the United States—including vaccines—have to gain approval from the U.S. Food and Drug Administration (FDA) before drug companies can sell them and doctors can prescribe them. The FDA's job is to make sure that drugs offered to patients are safe. Although the process can take a long time, the genital herpes vaccine may be available as early as 2008.

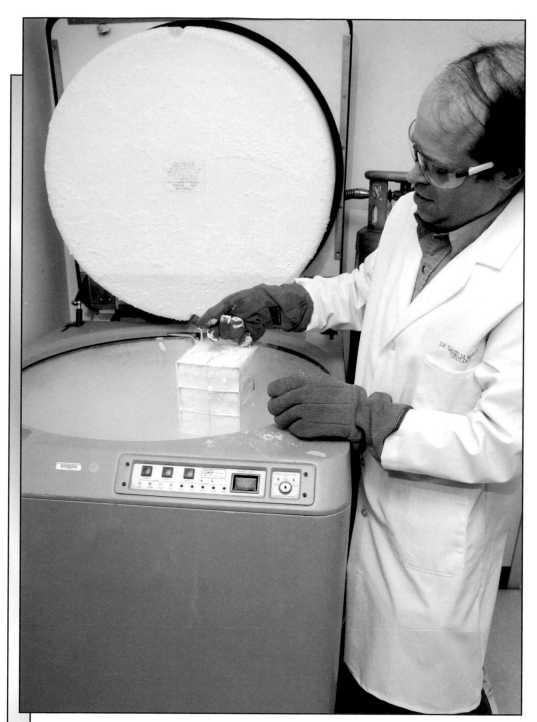

Researchers such as this doctor at the University of Wisconsin are trying to find ways to stop the spread of genital herpes. They don't expect to find a cure, but they are working on a vaccine that would keep people from getting the disease.

Scientists are also working to develop a gel that protects against the transmission of genital herpes. The gel blocks the virus from attaching itself to cells in a host organism. Results of the gel's effectiveness are expected in 2007.

Other scientists are trying to discover the causes of outbreaks later in life. At this point, it is a mystery why the disease stays hidden in the body for so long and suddenly appears at seemingly random times. Even though there are some triggers, the reasons why outbreaks happen when they do are not well understood.

CHAPTER FOUR

Preventing Genital Herpes

Genital herpes is spread through direct skin-to-skin contact with another person's genitals. A person with herpes is most contagious just before and during an outbreak. Your prevention strategy can't be based on knowing these two things, however. Remember: one person can pass the infection on to another even if no symptoms are present. So, how can you protect yourself? If you have genital herpes, how can you protect others?

ABSTINENCE: THE SAFEST BET

Abstinence means not having sex. To most people, this means not having vaginal intercourse. In the case of herpes, though, it's safest to take abstinence a step further. Genital herpes can be transmitted through any sexual contact. So, the only way to guarantee that you won't get the virus (or give it to someone else) is to abstain from all sexual contact—including anal sex, oral sex, and any other contact with another person's genitals.

Waiting to have sex until you are in a long-term relationship may reduce your risk. But, for many teens, this seems pretty far off. Still, a lot of teens choose abstinence. There are numerous ways to practice abstinence and still have a great romantic relationship.

How can you feel close to someone without having sex? It's easier than you might think. Watching a movie, cooking together, playing games, or even just talking are all ways to feel close. If you do want to get physical, there are options that won't expose you or your partner to

Not having any kind of sex—including oral and anal sex—is the only sure way to avoid STDs. Billboards, such as this one in Texas (*above*), help make this information available to a large number of people.

the risk. For example, hugging, cuddling, and kissing (as long as neither of you has a cold sore) are all safe. The most important thing is to set limits with your partner before you get physical. Discuss how far you want to go, and stick to your plan.

WHAT ABOUT CONDOMS?

When used correctly, latex condoms help protect against genital herpes, other STDs, and pregnancy. They are not 100-percent effective, however. This is especially true for preventing genital herpes. Contact with any infected skin that is not covered by the condom can still spread the disease. For example, a male with the genital herpes virus on his scrotum could pass the disease on to a female, even if he's wearing a condom.

Still, using condoms is one of the most important steps you can take to protect yourself and your partner during sexual contact. There are some important things to know about condoms:

- Condoms that are made of latex or polyurethane are more effective in preventing STDs and pregnancy than condoms made from other materials. (Some people are allergic to latex. If you have this kind of allergy, be sure to use polyurethane.)
- Condoms have expiration dates. This date is listed on the wrapper. Always check the date, and never use an expired condom.

- Heat can weaken condoms. Never keep them in your pockets, your wallet, or in your car.
- Never use lubricants that have oils in them (such as baby oil, lotions, or petroleum jelly) when using a condom. They can weaken condoms and make them more likely to break. Only water-based lubricants (such as KY Jelly) are safe to use with condoms.
- Don't use your teeth, scissors, or any other sharp object to open a condom wrapper. You might accidentally tear the condom.

Condoms can help protect against genital herpes, but only when they're used correctly. It is important to read the instructions on the packaging before use.

- Read and follow the instructions on the condom's packaging carefully. Know how to use a condom correctly before you run into a situation when you need one. Always put on a condom before you have *any* sexual contact.
- Be sure to use a new condom for each act of vaginal, anal, or oral sex. Never reuse condoms.

Talk to your doctor or another adult you trust if you have any questions about using condoms.

OTHER STEPS YOU CAN TAKE

If you do choose to be sexually active, condoms should be your first line of defense. But there are other things that can help you and your partner stay safe, too.

It is really important not to engage in any sexual contact during (or just before) an outbreak—even with a condom. This is the time when the genital herpes virus is most contagious. Plus, sex can irritate sores and make them take longer to heal. If you feel itching, tingling, or burning in an area where you had an outbreak before, there's a good chance another outbreak is about to begin. Stop having any kind of sex, and don't start again until at least a week after any sores heal. Here are some other tips:

- **Learn the facts about safer sex.** Know what methods will protect you from STDs and which ones won't. For example, a woman can contract or transmit genital herpes if she's on the Pill or if she uses a diaphragm. These methods protect only against pregnancy, not STDs.

- **Know what to look for.** Be ready to recognize the symptoms of genital herpes and other STDs. Talk to a doctor right away if you or your partner has any of the symptoms. But remember that many people may have an STD and not have any symptoms at all.

- **Talk openly and honestly with your partner.** Before you have any sexual contact, ask if he or she has ever had an STD, or if he or she has ever been

A health-care provider can be an excellent resource for information about safer sex, especially if you are not comfortable talking with your parents about sex.

tested. If your partner has or has had an STD, talk to a doctor right away. He or she will help you learn how to stay safe.

- **Oral sex and cold sores don't mix.** The herpes virus can be passed from a cold sore to a person's genitals. Don't perform oral sex if you have a cold sore, and don't receive oral sex if your partner has a cold sore.
- **Stay away from alcohol and other drugs.** Getting drunk or high will affect your judgment. You might be more likely to take risks, such as having unprotected sex or having sex with someone you don't know.

So, what's the bottom line? Always use condoms for any kind of sexual contact. Never engage in sexual contact when you or your partner is showing symptoms. Even more important, don't assume that you or your partner are herpes-free. If you know that you have genital herpes, talk to your partner before having sexual contact for the first time. Finally, you can take steps to reduce your chances of getting or spreading genital herpes. But the only way to be 100 percent safe is to practice abstinence. (Remember that abstinence means not engaging in oral, anal, or vaginal sex.)

SKILLS FOR SEXUAL HEALTH

You need more than facts to stay healthy and protect yourself from genital herpes and other STDs. You also

Doctors Are on Your Side

One of the best ways to stay healthy during your teen years is to see a doctor on a regular basis. In addition to going in for checkups, see your doctor right away if you think you have genital herpes or any other STD. Only your doctor can figure out whether you're infected. And only your doctor can prescribe medications if you need them. Early detection is crucial. A diagnosis means you can start treatment and begin taking steps to keep from spreading the infection to others.

need skills that can help you communicate, make good decisions, and set goals.

Having good communication skills is an important part of any relationship—especially one that might involve sex. You need to be able to talk to your partner about your sexual limits. You also need to talk about whether either of you might have an STD and if you should get tested. Poor communication skills could turn these conversations into arguments. But good communication skills will make your relationship even stronger.

One great technique involves using "I" statements. Using these statements can help set a tone that won't make your partner feel upset or defensive. What does that mean? Compare these two statements: "You're late for a date again! You're such a jerk!" and "I feel sad when you are late because it makes me feel like you don't care about me." Which one would you rather hear? Probably the second one. It lets you know how the other person feels, but it doesn't blame or accuse. Try to get in the habit of using "I" statements when you and your partner discuss your feelings. For example, you might say something like, "I really care about you, so I think we need to talk about using condoms."

Good communication skills also involve being able to say no when someone or something makes you feel uncomfortable. It's always your choice to say no to sexual contact. But it can be hard if someone you really like is

Talking openly and honestly with your partner plays a large part in protecting each other from genital herpes and other STDs. Good communication is also a great way to strengthen your relationship.

Ten Great Questions to Ask Your Doctor

A lot of people are uncomfortable talking about sex and their health. So, it helps to think about questions you have before you talk to your doctor. Here are some important questions to ask when you're seeking help:

1. What's the best way to protect myself from getting genital herpes?

2. I think I might have genital herpes. What are some symptoms to look out for? When should I get tested?

3. Do I have oral or genital herpes?

4. Does the test for genital herpes also check for other STDs?

5. Will I need to get tested for genital herpes again?

6. What's the best way to make sure I don't give genital herpes to someone else?

7. Does having genital herpes mean that I can never have sex?

8. How often will outbreaks occur? Will they always be as bad as the first one?

9. Will I be able to have kids someday?

10. Who are some other people who can help me?

pressuring you. All you have to do is be clear and direct. You can say something as simple as "I'm not ready yet" or "I don't want to get in trouble with my parents."

Being able to make good decisions is a big part of your sexual health. A lot of decisions can seem overwhelming.

It can help to break down the decision-making task into steps:

1. Define the problem. Figure out exactly what it is you're trying to decide. Be as specific as you can.
2. List your options. They don't all have to be practical. Write down whatever pops into your head. You might come up with a creative solution.
3. Make a list of pros and cons. For each option you listed in step two, write down any possible positive or negative outcomes.
4. Choose the best option. Which option has the most pros and the fewest cons? Use that to help you make your choice.
5. Evaluate the results. Think about how your decision worked out. How did your planning work? Were there any pros or cons that you didn't anticipate? Remembering these things could be useful the next time you need to make a similar decision.

Take your time when you need to make a big decision. Be calm and think things through as best you can. Don't make important decisions when you're angry or upset.

Learning how to set goals can also help you make good decisions, especially about sex. People usually set three different types of goals. Short-term goals are things you want to accomplish soon, such as in the next day or week. Medium-term goals are things you want to accomplish in the next few months, or even within the year. Long-term goals are things you want to accomplish more than a year from now.

Make a list of your short-, medium-, and long-term goals. When you're faced with a difficult decision, think about how your choice might affect your ability to reach your goals. For example, say you set a goal of receiving a sports scholarship to college. If you're trying to decide whether to have sex, think about how having a baby or catching an STD could affect your chances of reaching that goal.

Protecting yourself from STDs like genital herpes means that you need to be informed and be ready to stand up for your decisions. You—and only you—are in charge of your body. Staying healthy starts with the choices you make.

CHAPTER FIVE

Living with Genital Herpes

Nobody expects to catch a serious illness. Being diagnosed with a lifelong infection such as genital herpes can be overwhelming. People generally experience a wide range of emotions.

COMMON REACTIONS

In the first few months after a diagnosis, a lot of people feel sad, helpless, or hopeless. Some may even experience depression, which can be a severe condition. Coming to terms with the fact that there is no cure for genital herpes is difficult. These feelings are completely normal. But they don't have to last. Arming yourself with knowledge can be a big help. Learn as much about the disease as you can. For example, how can it spread and how can it be treated? Knowledge will help you understand how having herpes will affect your life. For many people, this means discovering that things maybe aren't as bad as they seem.

Some people feel embarrassed or ashamed. The fact that genital herpes is a sexually transmitted disease is the main reason they feel this way. They know that others will make assumptions about them. Therefore, many people try to keep their genital herpes a secret. That's fine—one's health is one's own business. But if you plan on having sex with someone, your herpes becomes his or her business, too. Telling your partner you have herpes *before* you have any sexual contact is extremely important. That way, you can both take steps to stay safe.

A diagnosis of genital herpes can be a big emotional burden. Counselors and support groups can help you deal with your feelings.

Anger is another common feeling. Sufferers may become mad at themselves for not taking the proper steps to prevent genital herpes. This type of guilt and self-blame can really hurt a person's self-esteem, making feelings of sadness or depression even worse. It's also common to be angry with the person who spread the disease. It may seem like this person was being careless or dishonest. Try to keep things in perspective and remember that some people with genital herpes don't even realize they have it.

HEALING FEELINGS

With time, feelings of anger or despair often go away—or at least fade. A good first step toward healing is to remind yourself that you didn't get genital herpes because you're a bad person. It's not a judgment or punishment. It's just a very common disease, and plenty of good people get it. Another thing to remember is that illness is a part of life. The idea that anyone is perfectly healthy is mostly a myth. Almost everyone experiences sickness, disease, or injury at one time or another. It's possible to be healthy and happy, even if you have genital herpes.

Here are a few other ways you can get on the road to emotional recovery:

- Keep telling yourself that your feelings are normal. Genital herpes isn't fatal, but it is a serious infection. Realizing that you have such an infection is a stressful situation, and that's OK. Having genital herpes doesn't mean that you won't be able to find many ways to enjoy life.

- Remember that treatments are available. They won't cure you, but they can make outbreaks less frequent and painful.
- Having genital herpes doesn't mean that you'll be unable to have a healthy sexual relationship. You will need to be open and honest with your sexual partners, however, and you'll need to educate yourself about taking steps for safer sex.

Counseling may be a great help. Through counseling, you will come to understand more about the disease and how to deal with your feelings. You'll also learn more about preventing the spread of genital herpes. A counselor can help you understand that the psychological impact of the disease may be more damaging than its physical impact.

GENITAL HERPES AND YOUR LOVE LIFE

Genital herpes can't kill you—but will it kill your love life? Not necessarily. Many people go on to have wonderful relationships after they've been diagnosed. Having genital herpes means that you'll face some unique challenges, though, and it means that you will have to be responsible. Being responsible doesn't require you to broadcast your disease to the whole world. But you need to be open and honest with any current or future sexual partner.

It might be hard to tell your partner that you have genital herpes, but it's the right thing to do. It is your responsibility to help stop the spread of genital herpes by letting your partner know your status before you have any sexual contact.

For example, if you're in a relationship when you find out you have genital herpes, you should talk with your partner when you feel ready (but before any sexual activity).

In addition to telling your current partner, it's important to talk to people you've had sexual contact with in the past. This isn't a witch hunt—don't act like you're on a mission to find out who gave you genital herpes. There's a good chance the person who gave you the disease doesn't even know he or she has it. By getting in touch with that person, you may be helping to protect his or her health—and the health of his or her future partners.

When you are in a new relationship, telling someone you have genital herpes can be tricky. Blurting out "I have genital herpes" on a first date probably won't go over too well. But holding off for a long time can make you feel like you're keeping a secret or, even worse, like you're lying. The one rule you should follow is to tell your partner *before* you have any kind of sexual contact. If you tell your partner after, he or she will probably feel betrayed and angry because you've exposed him or her to the disease. Talking about it may not be easy, but the advice that follows can help take the sting out of this otherwise unpleasant conversation.

First off, learn as much as you can about the disease. Learning the facts can prepare you to discuss your diagnosis with your partner. He or she is likely to have a lot of questions. Being able to answer those questions can help him or her feel better about the situation. Be ready to tell your partner the basic facts about how common the infection is, what it means to have it, and about any treatments you're receiving. Also, be prepared to show that you know how to take steps to keep from spreading the disease to your partner.

Second, try to pick an appropriate time and place. One thing is certain—the right time and place is not during the middle of a heavy make-out session. Start the discussion at a time when you won't be interrupted. Bringing up the subject while you're taking a walk or just hanging out and having a long conversation can help start things on the right foot.

When you feel like the time is right, be careful about the words you choose. Try to avoid projecting how you think your partner will react. Starting off by saying something like "This is really going to make you mad" or "You'll probably hate me for this" is almost a guarantee that the conversation won't go well. Also, avoid using negative words to describe the condition. For example, using words like "scary" or "gross" most likely won't make your partner feel very comfortable.

Try to stay positive. You might bring up the subject by saying, "I really like you. And I care about you a lot, so there's something I need to tell you before we get too serious." This approach reinforces all the good aspects of your relationship and can help your partner be more receptive to "bad" news. Another approach is to ask your partner if he or she has ever been tested for STDs. It might turn out that your partner needs to share exactly the same news with you.

Finally, prepare yourself for possible rejection. Your partner still might not react well to your news, even if you follow all of the advice provided in this book. Someone might break up with you as soon as he or she finds out. But another may be willing to accept you for who you are.

IF YOUR BOYFRIEND OR GIRLFRIEND HAS GENITAL HERPES

If you find out someone you've been dating has genital herpes, you may feel upset and a little scared. If you've already had sexual contact with the person, see your doctor right away. If you haven't had sexual contact—and you intend to continue dating the person—be sure to talk about how you will protect yourselves if or when you choose to be intimate.

People with genital herpes may need a lot of support. You can help your partner through a very difficult time. Be ready to talk about your partner's feelings and help the person feel like he or she can still be an attractive, happy individual.

If you've been dating for a while, you might suspect that your partner got genital herpes by cheating on you. Although this might be the case, it's just as likely that your partner had the disease before you met or started dating. Sometimes, people don't show symptoms for months or years after they've caught the infection.

RESOURCES

Whether you or somebody you know has genital herpes, it's important to know where to go for help. A doctor is always a good choice. He or she will be able to test you if you think you've been exposed to the virus. Doctors can also prescribe drugs to help treat the disease.

    If you're not comfortable talking to your parents or another family member, consider bringing your concerns

Doctors can test you for genital herpes and prescribe drugs to help prevent outbreaks. They are also a helpful resource. But there are other adults you can talk to as well. For example, you could talk to a parent, a coach, or a teacher.

Mercedes' Story

It all started when Kelvin asked Mercedes out. He was good looking—and he was also smart, funny, and sweet. All of Mercedes' girlfriends were jealous.

Things got serious pretty fast. He seemed so perfect, and she really fell for him. They ended up having sex a few times. Mercedes was already taking the Pill to make her periods more regular. She wasn't worried about getting pregnant, so she didn't ask him to use a condom. Kelvin was her first sexual partner. He said Mercedes was his first, too.

About two weeks after they first had sex, Mercedes started to feel a weird itching sensation in her vagina. She thought it was a yeast infection, but pretty soon sores started to appear. She didn't know what was wrong with her. At first, she didn't want to ask her parents. What would they say if they found out she was having sex? But she finally talked to her mom, who made an appointment for Mercedes to see a doctor.

Mercedes couldn't believe it when the doctor said it looked like she had genital herpes. "How can that be?" Mercedes asked. "I thought only girls who slept around got that." The doctor said genital herpes can happen to anyone and suggested that Mercedes talk to her boyfriend. Explaining that he may not know he had the infection, the doctor said she'd have to run some tests to make sure. She said Kelvin should also get tested right away.

Mercedes talked to Kelvin. It turned out that he'd had a fling with another girl the summer before he met Mercedes. But he couldn't bring himself to tell her. He was ashamed of what he'd done, and he said he was worried Mercedes would break up with him if she knew the truth. He was shocked that he'd given her genital herpes. He'd never had an outbreak. After Mercedes and Kelvin talked, he went to the doctor and got tested, too.

When the results came back, both Mercedes and Kelvin tested positive for the infection. On Mercedes' second visit, the doctor prescribed some medicine. They also had a long talk about how to make sex safer. Mercedes learned a lot about using condoms—including the fact that not even condoms are a guarantee that you won't get an STD like genital herpes.

Mercedes certainly wasn't happy to find out that she'd have genital herpes for the rest of her life. But she was glad she went to the doctor when she did. The doctor said the drugs will help Mercedes have fewer outbreaks. And Mercedes learned how to avoid giving the infection to someone else, which she definitely doesn't want to happen.

to a teacher, coach, or any other adult you trust. You might also ask about support groups at your local hospital.

Finally, there are hotlines and Web sites where you can get advice and information. Several are listed in the back of this book. One of the most popular is the National Herpes Hotline: (919) 361-8488. The hotline is open from 9:00 AM to 6:00 PM (EST) Monday through Friday. Once armed with resources, information, and support, you will be well on your way toward dealing with genital herpes.

GLOSSARY

abstinence The practice of not having any kind of sexual contact, including vaginal, anal, or oral sex.

Cesarean section A type of surgery in which a doctor cuts into a woman's abdomen to remove her baby. The surgery is usually performed when a vaginal birth would be dangerous for the baby or the mother.

cold sore A painful, fluid-filled blister that usually appears on a person's lips or near the mouth. Cold sores are caused by the herpes simplex 1 (HSV-1) virus. They are also called fever blisters.

genitals The sexual organs (including a man's penis and testicles, and a woman's vulva and clitoris) on the outside of a person's body.

HIV (human immunodeficiency virus) The virus that causes AIDS (acquired immunodeficiency syndrome). HIV attacks the body's immune system, making it harder to fight off other illnesses and diseases.

immune system A system of cells in a person's body that kills germs and fights diseases.

latex A type of very thin rubber that is used to make condoms.

reproduction The creation of new life, such as when a virus multiplies or when two people make a baby.

STDs (sexually transmitted diseases) Diseases that can be passed from person to person through sexual contact. They are also called STIs (sexually transmitted infections).

symptom A sign of a disease or illness. For example, bumps or blisters on the genitals can be a symptom of genital herpes.

transmission The process of spreading a disease from one person to another.

vaccine A type of medicine that prevents a person from getting a disease.

viral shedding In the case of genital herpes, viral shedding refers to the period of time when the virus is present on the surface of the infected person's skin. This means that the disease can be passed to another person.

virus A very tiny germ that infects and damages the cells of a larger organism, such as an animal or a person.

FOR MORE INFORMATION

American Herpes Foundation
433 Hackensack Avenue
Hackensack, NJ 07601
(201) 342-4441
Web site: http://www.herpes-foundation.org
A nonprofit organization that offers information and
education about herpes.

American Social Health Association (ASHA)
Herpes Resource Center/National Herpes Hotline
P.O. Box 13827
Research Triangle Park, NC 27709
(919) 361-8488
Web site: http://www.ashastd.org
ASHA's trained health communication specialists provide
information about the transmission, prevention, and
treatment of the herpes simplex virus. Hotline available
9:00 AM to 6:00 PM (EST), Monday through Friday.

Centers for Disease Control and Prevention (CDC)
1600 Clifton Road
Atlanta, GA 30333
(800) CDC-INFO (232-4636)

Web site: http://www.cdc.gov
The CDC provides anonymous, confidential information on many health topics, including sexually transmitted diseases, twenty-four hours a day, seven days a week.

The Phoenix Association
Genital Herpes Support Group
4936 Yonge Street, Suite 134
Toronto, ON M2N 6S3
Canada
(416) 449-0876
Web site: http://www.torontoherpes.com
A volunteer-run organization that offers support groups and information for people with genital herpes. Calls are returned in the evenings and on weekends.

Public Health Agency of Canada
130 Colonnade Road
A.L. 6501H
Ottawa, ON K1A 0K9
Canada
(866) 225-0709 (within Canada); (613) 957-2991 (outside of Canada)
Web site: http://www.phac-aspc.gc.ca
A federal agency with the mission of preventing injuries and chronic diseases, and responding to public health emergencies and infectious disease outbreaks. Offers information on a wide range of health and safety issues.

WEB SITES

Due to the changing nature of Internet links, the Rosen Publishing Group, Inc., has developed an online list of Web sites related to the subject of this book. This site is updated regularly. Please use this link to access the list:

http://www.rosenlinks.com/lsh/gehe

FOR FURTHER READING

Bailey, Jacqui. *Sex, Puberty and All That Stuff: A Guide to Growing Up*. New York, NY: Barron's, 2004.

Ford, Jean. *Right on Schedule! A Teen's Guide to Growth and Development* (The Science of Health: Youth and Well Being). Philadelphia, PA: Mason Crest Publishers, 2005.

Kolesnikow, Tassia. *Sexually Transmitted Diseases* (Diseases and Disorders). San Diego, CA: Lucent Books, 2003.

Marr, Lisa. *Sexually Transmitted Diseases: A Physician Tells You What You Need to Know*. Baltimore, MD: The Johns Hopkins University Press, 1998.

Sacks, Stephen L. *The Truth About Herpes*, 4th ed. Seattle, WA: Gordon Soules Book Publishers Ltd., 1997.

Shaw, Tucker, and Fiona Gibb. *This Book Is About Sex* (Alloy Books). New York, NY: Puffin Books, 2000.

Shoquist, Jennifer, and Diane Stafford. *The Encyclopedia of Sexually Transmitted Diseases* (Facts on File Library of Health and Living). New York, NY: Facts On File, Inc., 2004.

Silverstein, Alvin, Virginia B. Silverstein, and Laura Silverstein Nunn. *The STDs Update* (Disease Update). Berkeley Heights, NJ: Enslow Publishers, 2005.

Spencer, Juliet V. *Herpes* (Deadly Diseases and Epidemics). Philadelphia, PA: Chelsea House Publishers, 2005.

Stanberry, Lawrence R. *Understanding Herpes* (Understanding Health and Sickness), 2nd ed. Jackson, MS: University Press of Mississippi, 2006.

Stanley, Deborah A., ed. *Sexual Health Information for Teens: Health Tips about Sexual Development, Human Reproduction, and Sexually Transmitted Diseases* (Teen Health Series). Detroit, MI: Omnigraphics, 2003.

BIBLIOGRAPHY

American Social Health Association. "Herpes Simplex Virus (HSV)—Overview." Retrieved December 28, 2005 (http://www.iwannaknow.org/basics2/herpes.html).

Bailey, Jacqui. *Sex, Puberty and All That Stuff: A Guide to Growing Up*. New York, NY: Barron's, 2004.

Centers for Disease Control and Prevention. "Genital Herpes." Retrieved December 28, 2005 (http://www.cdc.gov/std/Herpes/default.htm).

Marr, Lisa. *Sexually Transmitted Diseases: A Physician Tells You What You Need to Know*. Baltimore, MD: The Johns Hopkins University Press, 1998.

National Institutes of Health. "Genital Herpes." Retrieved December 28, 2005 (http://www.niaid.nih.gov/factsheets/stdherp.htm).

Nourse, Alan E. *Herpes*. New York, NY: Franklin Watts, 1985.

Planned Parenthood. "Herpes—Questions and Answers." Retrieved December 28, 2005 (http://www.plannedparenthood.org/pp2/portal/files/portal/medicalinfo/sti/pub-sti-herpes.xml).

Shoquist, Jennifer, and Diane Stafford. "Genital Herpes." *The Encyclopedia of Sexually Transmitted Diseases*. New York, NY: Facts On File, 2004.

TeensHealth. "Genital Herpes." Retrieved December 28, 2005 (http://www.kidshealth.org/teen/sexual_health/stds/std_herpes.html).

WomensHealth.gov. "Genital Herpes." Retrieved December 28, 2005 (http://www.4woman.gov/faq/stdherpe.htm).

INDEX

ABOUT THE AUTHOR

Since graduating from college with degrees in English and economics, Greg Saulmon has written extensively about public health and safety. His work includes pieces on dating and relationships, the health-care system, and sexually transmitted diseases. He lives in western Massachusetts with his wife.

PHOTO CREDITS

Designer: Nelson Sá; **Editor:** Elizabeth Gavril
Photo Researcher: Amy Feinberg